INTERMEDIATE GRAMMAR WORKBOOK 2

SYLVIA CHALKER

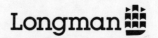

Longman Group UK Limited,
*Longman House, Burnt Mill, Harlow,
Essex CM20 2JE, England
and Associated Companies throughout the world*

© Longman Group UK Limited 1987

*All rights reserved; no part of this publication
may be reproduced, stored in a retrieval system,
or transmitted in any form or by any means, electronic,
mechanical, photocopying, recording or otherwise,
without the prior written permission of the Publishers.*

First published 1987
Sixth impression 1991

ISBN 0-582-97605-7

Set in 10/12 Palatino

Produced by Longman Singapore Publishers Pte Ltd
Printed in Singapore

Acknowledgements

We are grateful to the following for permission to reproduce copyright photographs:

Associated Press Ltd for page 17; BBC Hulton Picture Library for page 29; Peter Francis/Camera Press Ltd for page 31; The J. Allan Cash Photolibrary for page 10; Kalem/The Kobal Collection for page 23; Pixfeatures for page 58; Popperfoto for page 22.

We are indebted to Thames Television Ltd for permission to use an adapted version of a trick from *David Nixon's Magic Box*.

Illustrations by Mark Peppé

CONTENTS

SECTION 1 DETERMINERS AND PRONOUNS
1.1 Possessives: *my, mine*
1.2 *A friend of mine*
1.3 *An apple a day*
1.4 *Some* or *any*: *A trick with paper*
1.5 *Anything, everyone, somebody, nowhere*
1.6 *Much, many, a lot*: *A holiday in Portugal*
1.7 *A few, a little, very few, very little*

SECTION 2 NOUNS
2.1 Mass or count nouns: *in hospital* or *in a hospital?*
2.2 Plurals: *Fascinating facts*
2.3 Singular or plural?

SECTION 3 VERBS: TIME AND TENSE
3.1 Present progressive: *What are they all doing?*
3.2 Present progressive: *Are you doing anything next week?*
3.3 Asking questions: *Jogging*
3.4 Present perfect: *been, come* or *gone?*
3.5 Present perfect: *Have you read any good books lately?*
3.6 Past simple: Pronunciation of regular *–ed*
3.7 *Since, for, ago*: *Games*

SECTION 4 AUXILIARIES AND MODALS
4.1 Future opportunity: *can*
4.2 Past ability: *Two daring people*
4.3 Requests and invitations: *could* and *would*
4.4 Advice: *What had he better do?*
4.5 *Have you got . . . ? Do you have . . . ? Are you having . . . ?*
4.6 *What will he be doing?*
4.7 Will DO or will be DOING: *In the travel agent's*

SECTION 5 ADJECTIVES AND ADVERBS

5.1 Some adjectives and adverbs: *The same word or different?*

5.2 Comparison of adjectives: *The Sinclair C5*

5.3 Comparatives and superlatives: *Some world records*

5.4 Position of time adverbials: *often? every day?*

5.5 *Enough money, young enough: Hang-gliding*

SECTION 6 PREPOSITIONS

6.1 Some prepositions of place: *The Trans-Siberian Railway*

6.2 *Over* and *above*

6.3 *Under* and *below*

6.4 A trick: *The pin in the bottle*

6.5 An acrostic: *Opposites*

SECTION 7 PHRASAL VERBS

7.1 *Down, off, on, out*

7.2 *Up: Andrew and Rachel*

7.3 Prepositional verbs: *The suitcase*

SECTION 8 VERB PATTERNS

8.1 Verbs of perception: *I saw him run/running*

8.2 *Agree to DO, consider DOING*

8.3 *Let, make: What do the notices mean?*

8.4 Indirect objects: *to* or *for?*

8.5 Infinitives: *Careers*

SECTION 9 COMPLEX SENTENCES

9.1 True conditions: *Snakes and ladders*

9.2 Conditions: *Future possibilities*

9.3 Conditions: *If only things were different now!*

9.4 Wishing: *She wishes things were different now*

9.5 Wishing about the future: *Things could be different one day*

9.6 More relative clauses

9.7 Relative clauses with prepositions at the end

9.8 Relative clauses: *who, which, whose*

9.9 What to do: *A crash survivor*

SECTION 1   DETERMINERS AND PRONOUNS

1.1 Possessives: *my, mine*

This That	is	my our your his her their	car.		It's	mine. ours. yours. his. hers. theirs.
These Those	are		cars.		They're	

Complete the following with the right possessive word.

MINOJI   Is this guitar ¹_____, Gudrun?

GUDRUN   No, that's not ²_____. This is ³_____ guitar here.

MINOJI   Is this Marie-Christine's car?

GUDRUN   Heavens no! That's ⁴_____ over there.

MINOJI   So who does this car belong to? Is it Suleiman's?

GUDRUN   Well, it's not ⁵_____ exactly. It's ⁶_____ father's.

SULEIMAN   Is this ⁷_____ walkman, Olga?

OLGA   Yes, that's ⁸_____. It's ⁹_____ most

              valuable possession.

DAVID GREEN   Gudrun, Marie-Christine, Suleiman, everybody! Come and collect

              ¹⁰_____ passports.

STUDENTS   Those aren't ¹¹_____. We've already got

              ¹²_____ passports.

JUAN   Are those Bob and Susan's children?

STEPHAN   No, no. Those aren't ¹³_____ children.

              ¹⁴_____ are older. Here's a picture of Andrew and Rachel.

JUAN   And who are they? Is one of them Wendy's mother?

SOFIA   Yes, that's ¹⁵_____ mother on the left, with one of

              ¹⁶_____ friends.

5

DETERMINERS AND PRONOUNS

1.2 *A friend of mine*

> He is *a friend of mine/ours*. ONE OF MY/OUR FRIENDS

Complete the following, using *of* + *mine*, *ours* etc.

SOFIA   Have you ever read one of Juan's short stories?
STEPHAN   Yes, I read a very clever story ¹_____ the other day.

SUSAN   Bob! It's time to go!
BOB   Right! But where on earth are those children ⁴_____?

WENDY   Do you know any of Olga's Polish friends?
DAVID   Yes. I met some friends ²_____ at that barbecue.

OLGA   That's one of my favourite records.
GUDRUN   Yes, it's a favourite ⁵_____ too.

JUAN   I met Michael Lever at David and Wendy's the other day.
SULEIMAN   Oh. He's a neighbour ³_____, isn't he?

MARIE-CHRISTINE   I've got a book ⁶_____ at home.
MINOJI   Oh good. It's not mine. It's a library book, actually.

6

DETERMINERS AND PRONOUNS

1.3 *An apple a day*

> An apple *a day*
> Keeps the doctor away!

A This old saying means that apples are so healthy that if you eat an apple a day (one apple every day), you will not need the doctor! Here are some more phrases with *a* + 'measure words'. Can you match them up to make some sensible sentences?

1000 miles (1480 km) an hour	54.4 hours a week
5 million barrels of oil a day	once a month
32.3 hours a week	70 miles an hour
a mile a minute	US$ 850 an ounce (US$ 29.98 a gram)
twice a day	233 pounds (106 kilos) of potatoes a year

1 The moon goes round the earth approximately _____
2 In 1980 the price of gold reached _____
3 The average South Korean worked _____ in 1983.
4 The speed limit on motorways in Britain is _____
5 The average Briton eats _____
6 The average Finn, in 1983, worked _____
7 There's a plant that grows so fast it is called _____
8 The two hands of a clock are both together at 12 _____
9 People living on the Equator move at _____
10 Saudi Arabia produces _____

B What about you and your friends?
How many cups of coffee/cans of cola do you drink a day/a week?
How many kilometres do you walk a month/a year?
How many hours do you work/study a week?
How many hours of television do you watch a day/a week/a month?

11 I drink _____ a day.
12 My friend _____ a _____
13 I walk _____ a _____
14 He/She _____
15 I work/study _____
16 He/She _____
17 I _____
18 He/She _____

7

DETERMINERS AND PRONOUNS

1.4 *Some* or *any*: A trick with paper

Quantity or amount				
Questions and negative	Have you No I haven't	any	books. matches.	Countable plural
Questions and positive	Would you like I can give you	some	paper. string.	Mass

Identity	
Some tricks are easy; others aren't. SOME, BUT NOT OTHERS *Any tricks* – even easy ones – need practice. ANY KIND WHATEVER	Countable plural
Some mean person has spoilt my trick. A PARTICULAR PERSON You can use *any book* for this trick. ANY KIND WHATEVER	Countable singular
Some paper is made from wood, and some from old paper. SOME KINDS, BUT NOT OTHERS You can use *any paper* for this trick. ANY KIND WHATEVER	Mass

Complete the following by using *some* or *any*.

¹ _Some_____ clever person – I forget who now – once showed me ² _____ very good tricks. Of course ³ _____ good trick needs ⁴ _____ practice, but there are ⁵ _____ tricks that are difficult to do if you cannot find ⁶ _____ of the things you need.

But for this trick that I'm going to describe now you don't need ⁷ _____ expensive things at all. All you need are ⁸ _____ books and ⁹ _____ paper. ¹⁰ _____ paper will do as long as it is reasonably strong. The trick is to make a tube of paper hold up ¹¹ _____ heavy books (as in the picture.) Have you ¹² _____ idea why this works? (Stephan says he hasn't ¹³ _____ idea at all, but Gudrun has ¹⁴ _____ idea.)

Don't believe ¹⁵ _____ clever person who says it can't be done, because it can. Roll the paper into a tube and hold it together with ¹⁶ _____ string. Then pile on ¹⁷ _____ books, one at a time. ¹⁸ _____ books are suitable, though it is more difficult with very large books.

Of course the tube will fall down eventually – but it's a good trick.

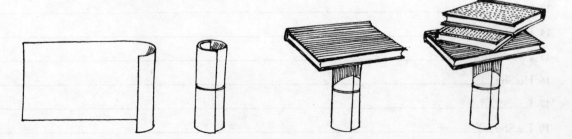

1.5 Anything, everyone, somebody, nowhere

> ▲ Have you asked *anybody*?
>
> *Somebody* must know the answer.
>
> ■ I've asked *everybody*.
>
> But *nobody* knows a thing about it.

A Complete the following using *anything, everything, nothing, something*.

▲ You must have heard at least [1] *something*.

■ No, people don't tell me [2]_____. I know absolutely [3]_____ not a thing. [4]_____ is a complete secret.

Now complete the following using *anyone, everyone, no one, someone*

▲ [5]_____ knows the earth is round.

■ Do they? [6]_____ told me that there's a flat earth society, and the members all say that the earth is flat!

▲ Oh, [7]_____ could possibly believe that. [8]_____ who says that is mad.

Now use *anywhere, everywhere, nowhere* and *somewhere* to complete these.

▲ Where's the tin-opener? I can't see it [9]_____.

■ Well, it must be [10]_____.

▲ But I've looked [11]_____. There's [12]_____ else to look.

B Now complete the following using any of the words you have used in 1–12.

It is such a small village that [13]_____ knows [14]_____ else. Some people say that there's [15]_____ special to do and [16]_____ to go. But I find there is always [17]_____ interesting happening. Personally I can't think of [18]_____ nicer to live than a village. There is [19]_____ so good about fresh air. I don't think [20]_____ could disagree.

DETERMINERS AND PRONOUNS

1.6 *Much, many, a lot: A holiday in Portugal*

How many rooms *are there?*	*How much* furniture *is there?*
There aren't many (rooms).	*There isn't much* (furniture).
There are a lot (of rooms).	*There is a lot* (of furniture).

Gudrun has invited Olga to join her and two other friends for a holiday in Portugal. Olga is telephoning her to find out more details about the villa Gudrun wants to rent. Fill in the conversation with *How many . . . are there?* or one of the other alternatives in the table.

OLGA   How ¹_____ rooms _____?

GUDRUN   There ²_____. In fact, only two bedrooms and a sitting-room, but they are large. And of course there's a kitchen and a shower-room.

OLGA   Only two bedrooms! How ³_____ beds _____?

GUDRUN   Oh, there ⁴_____ beds – five, I think. Two in each bedroom and a spare one in the sitting-room.

OLGA   Is it a nice sitting-room? How ⁵_____ furniture _____?

GUDRUN   Well, there ⁶_____ – just a table and four chairs.

OLGA   Well, I expect we could manage. Tell me about the place though.

GUDRUN   There ⁷_____ beaches, and . . .

OLGA   But how ⁸_____ sand _____? – or is it really all rocky?

GUDRUN   Oh, all that part of Portugal is sandy – you'll love it.

OLGA   But will we get good weather? How ⁹_____ hours of sunshine _____ a day in August? And how ¹⁰_____ rain _____ in that part of Portugal?

GUDRUN   Goodness, Olga! There ¹¹_____ sunshine – hours and hours. And there ¹²_____ rain – often no rain at all. It'll be lovely.

10

DETERMINERS AND PRONOUNS

1.7 *A few, a little, very few, very little*

> There are *a few* aspirins.
> There is *a little* shampoo.   PERHAPS ENOUGH
>
> There are *very few* aspirins.
> There is *very little* shampoo.   NOT ENOUGH, ALMOST NONE

Olga is thinking about her holiday and looking in her cupboard. She hasn't got much of anything on her list! She puts a question mark(?) where there are *a few* or there is *a little* (in other words, where she has perhaps got enough). But she puts a cross (X) where there are *very few* or there is *very little*, and she needs some more. Write out what she thinks, using the words on her list.

```
1 aspirins x         5 sun oil x
2 shampoo ?          6 soap ?
3 toothpaste x       7 sweets ?
4 paper
  handkerchiefs ?    8 films x
                       (for camera)
```

1   *There are very few aspirins.*
2   *There is a little shampoo.*
3   _____
4   _____
5   _____
6   _____
7   _____
8   _____

SECTION 2 NOUNS

2.1 Mass or count nouns: *in hospital* or *in a hospital?*

Tom is *in hospital*.	Tom is *in a modern hospital*.
Sometimes he sleeps *by day/at night*.	Wendy works *in a hospital*.
	Sometimes she sleeps *in/during the day/the morning*.

Insert *a* or *the* where necessary, or leave blank(∅). In a few places two answers are possible.

▲ Is Suleiman still at [1]_____ school?

■ No, he's left [2]_____ school. He enjoyed being at [3]_____ good school, but he'd had enough. He goes to [4]_____ university now.

There are thousands of people in [5]_____ prison all over the world. Wendy's mother works in [6]_____ prison – she teaches there.

▲ Where's Rachel?

■ She went to [7]_____ bed with a temperature, but now she's sitting up in [8]_____ bed feeling much better, and with toys all over [9]_____ bed.

Wendy does shift work at [10]_____ local hospital. This means that she sometimes has to work at [11]_____ night and try to sleep by [12]_____ day. Sometimes she feels tired during [13]_____ night, but she cannot always get to sleep in [14]_____ day. She says, 'I usually stay up in [15]_____ morning, and go to [16]_____ bed in [17]_____ afternoon.'

▲ Some people say we ought to get up at [18]_____ sunrise and go to bed at [19]_____ sunset.

■ Well, I couldn't possibly do that. But did you see [20]_____ sunrise yesterday? It was beautiful.

▲ Goodnight! Sleep well. See you at [21]_____ breakfast.

■ I wonder what they'll give us for [22]_____ breakfast. I always like [23]_____ big breakfast.

▲ Can you come to [24]_____ dinner with us on Saturday?

■ Oh, I'm sorry, no. We're going to [25]_____ farewell dinner at the Castle Hotel for one of Wendy's friends who is leaving.

2.2 Plurals: *Fascinating facts*

Common irregular plurals		man/men foot/feet penny/pence or pennies
Zero plurals		cod/cod fish/fish(es) sheep/sheep aircraft/aircraft
-is		analysis/analyses
-f or *-fe*	irregular	wife/wives scarf/scarves or scarfs
	regular	belief/beliefs proof/proofs
-o	irregular	hero/heroes tomato/tomatoes mosquito/mosquitoes or mosquitos
	regular	radio/radios zoo/zoos
Compounds	irregular	sister-in-law/sisters-in-law
	regular	grown-up/grown-ups sit-in/sit-ins

Complete the following with the plural forms of the words shown in *italics*.

1 *oasis* There are some green __oases__ in the Sahara Desert.

2 *cliff* The highest sea _____ in the world are in the Hawaiian islands.

3 *hovercraft* _____ cross the English Channel between France and England in under an hour.

4 *policewoman* Years ago there were only men in the police; now there are also _____.

5 *sheep* You do not see _____ on a menu. _____ are animals; the meat is called mutton or lamb.

6 *goose* Many farmers find it easier to keep chickens than _____.

7 *potato* Crisps and chips are made from _____.

8 *brother-in-law* If your husband or wife has a brother, and your sister is married, then you have two _____.

9 *loaf* The best _____ come from a baker's, not a supermarket.

10 *cod, fish* _____ are round _____.

11 *penny* You can put ten _____ in a public telephone, but you cannot use ten separate _____.

12 *handkerchief* Hankies is an informal word for _____.

13 *spaceman* Perhaps we shall all be _____ by the year 2000.

14 *volcano* There are active _____ in many parts of the world.

15 *shelf* Even in a small earthquake pictures fall off walls and books fall off _____.

16 *kangaroo, zoo* Outside Australia, most _____ are in _____.

17 *lay-by* There are special _____ on main roads where you can stop.

18 *hoof, roof* Horses have _____; houses have _____.

19 *take-away* Shops that sell cooked meals to eat at home are called _____.

20 *life, crisis* Some people's _____ seem to be full of _____.

2.3 Singular or plural?

		Plural or singular verb?
Plural not ending in s	The police_ (Some) people_	are ...
Plural only but not countable	The ⎱ clothe<u>s</u> Some ⎰ belongings thank<u>s</u>	are ...
Plural only: not countable alone **countable with *pair***	The ⎱ trouser<u>s</u> Some ⎰ jean<u>s</u> This pair of glasses Three pairs of trousers	are ... are ... is ... are ...
Mass	This ⎱ new<u>s</u> Some ⎰	is ...

Choose the right words in the following.

- ■ Some people [1] *has/have* found your things, and the police [2] *say/says* that you can collect them at the police station.
- ▲ Oh marvellous. I hope all my belongings [3] *are/is* there.
- ■ Well, there [4] *are/is* a pair of trousers. There are also [5] *three/some* jeans. And there are two [6] *glasses/pairs of glasses*.
- ▲ That [7] *are/is* good news.
- ■ [8] *Was/Were* there any other clothes?
- ▲ No, but I also dropped [9] *a/some* scissors.
- ■ The police didn't mention scissors.
- ▲ Well, never mind. My thanks [10] *are/is* due to you and everybody for all your help.

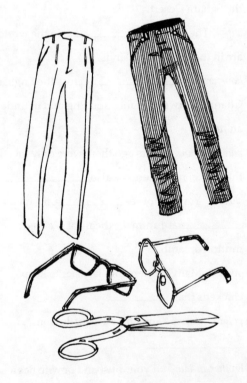

SECTION 3 VERBS: TIME AND TENSE

3.1 Present progressive: *What are they all doing?*

8 a.m. Wednesday	Venezuela:	Juan – have breakfast
12 noon	Iceland:	Magnus – call Minoji
	England:	Wendy and her mother – shop
1 p.m.	France:	Marie-Christine – work
	Poland:	Olga – have lunch
	Sweden:	Gudrun – study
	Switzerland:	Stephan – ski
2 p.m.	Greece:	Sofia – teach
3 p.m.	Saudi Arabia:	Suleiman – study
9 p.m.	Japan:	Minoji – watch TV
1 a.m. Thursday	New Zealand:	Wendy's brother – sleep

It is 12 noon in England on Wednesday 20th January. Wendy is wondering what all those students who were in David's class last year are doing at this moment. You can tell her! Complete the following using the present progressive tense.

1 While Wendy _is wondering_ about the students, Sofia _is teaching_.

2 While Stephan _____, Marie-Christine _____.

3 While Minoji _____, Magnus _____ him on his radio.

4 Juan _____ in Venezuela, while Olga _____ in Poland.

5 While Suleiman _____ in Saudi Arabia, Gudrun also _____ at home in Sweden.

6 While Wendy and her mother _____, her brother in New Zealand _____.

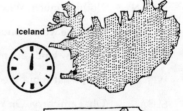

15

VERBS: TIME AND TENSE

3.2 Present progressive: *Are you doing anything next week?*

Here is Susan's diary for next week. Complete the conversation, using information from the diary. Use these verbs (in the present progressive):

1 do
2 go
3 have
4 meet
5 see
6 have
7 go
8 meet
9 take
10 do

SUN 14
6 pm school concert

MON 15
4 pm meet Tom – Heathrow

TUES 16
3 Rachel & Andrew to dentist

WED 17
7 Dinner with Bob's mother

THURS 18
1 o'clock lunch – Janet
2 – hairdresser's

FRI 19
7.30 meet Bob – Odeon
A Passage to India

SAT 20

Notes

WENDY   ¹ _Are_ you _doing_ anything next week?

SUSAN   Nothing much. Why?

WENDY   Well, we were wondering if you could all come to dinner on Sunday evening.

SUSAN   Oh, how kind. But no. We ² _____ to the _____ then.

WENDY   Well what about Wednesday evening? – or Friday?

SUSAN   Oh, I am sorry. On Wednesday we ³ _____ _____ and on Friday I ⁴ _____ Bob and we ⁵ _____ _____.

WENDY   Well, is there any chance of just seeing you next week, Susan? Could you come to tea on Monday or Tuesday, say? Or what about Thursday lunch?

SUSAN   Oh this is awful. Thursday's definitely no good, because I ⁶ _____ with a friend, and then I ⁷ _____ to the _____. Monday's hopeless, because I ⁸ _____ at _____, and Tuesday's just as bad because I ⁹ _____ to the _____. But listen – we ¹⁰ _____ n't _____ anything on Saturday 20th. How about you two coming to dinner with us? Will you?

3.3 Asking questions: *Jogging*

Practise asking questions by writing out in full the questions below. They must make sense with the answers given. Use simple and progressive tenses, past or present. We have done the first one for you.

1 ▲ (You/*know*) the name Jim Fixx?

Do you know the name Jim Fixx?

● Yes, I do. He was an American millionaire and a jogger.

2 ▲ How (he/*become*) a millionaire?

● Through his books on jogging and all the publicity.

3 ▲ (What/*happen*) to him?

● He died in July 1984 at the age of 52.

4 ▲ What (he/*do*) when (he/*die*)?

● He was out jogging.

5 ▲ (People/immediately/*stop*) jogging?

● No. Most people just went on jogging.

6 ▲ How much (some people/*jog*)?

● Some jog 100 miles a week.

7 ▲ And when (most people/*jog*)?

● Often before breakfast.

8 ▲ (Regular exercise/*not do*) the heart good?

● Yes, but jogging can be dangerous if you're older or not very fit.

9 ▲ (Jogging/actually/ever/*cause*) heart attacks?

● Many people think it does.

10 ▲ And (what sort of evidence/*emerge*) now to prove that jogging is good for you?

● You must ask the joggers!

11 ▲ (Who/*want*) to die young?

● Nobody!

VERBS: TIME AND TENSE

3.4 Present perfect: *been, come* or *gone*?

> David *has gone* to school today. HE IS THERE NOW.
> David and Wendy *have been* to France.   THEY ARE *NOT* THERE NOW. THEY CAME/HAVE COME BACK.
> The postman *has come*.   HE IS HERE NOW.
> The postman *has been*.   HE IS *NOT* HERE NOW – HE HAS GONE AGAIN. BUT THE POST IS HERE!

Complete the following, using *has/have* + *been/come/gone*.

It is 9 a.m. on Thursday morning, and there is nobody at David and Wendy's, except the cat, which ¹ *has come* in from the garden. They ² _____ both _____ to work. David is already teaching. Wendy ³ _____ just _____ to the hospital. Her mother ⁴ _____ to stay for a few days, but she ⁵ _____ now _____ home. (She left yesterday.)

It's 10 o'clock now. And what is happening at Bob and Susan's? Well, Bob ⁶ _____ already _____ to his office, but he

⁷ _____ home to pick up some papers. Andrew isn't here. He ⁸ _____ to school, but Rachel ⁹ _____ n't _____ because she's ill. (Look at those spots!) She has been at home all the week, and the doctor ¹⁰ _____ to see her. In fact he's coming again today. Susan ¹¹ _____ just _____ out to the shops, but she's back now.

4 p.m. and the doctor ¹² _____ at last. But Rachel's spots ¹³ _____ ! (Where are they?) She is much better.

8 p.m. David ¹⁴ _____ home, and he and Wendy have had dinner. But he ¹⁵ _____ out again to a teachers' meeting. It's a hard life!

VERBS: TIME AND TENSE

3.5 Present perfect: *Have you read any good books lately?*

A Work with a friend. Ask each other questions using the verbs given. First write your questions. Then ask and answer, using *Yes, I have* or *No, I haven't*.

Have you read any good books lately?	Yes, I have. No, I haven't.

1 *write* ___Have you written___ a letter to anyone *recently*?
2 *eat* _____ any chocolate *today*?
3 *go* _____ to the cinema *this week*?
4 *read* _____ an English story book *in the last few weeks*?
5 *buy* _____ anything *since last week*?
6 *go* _____ abroad *in the last few years*?
7 *grow out of* _____ your clothes *in the past year*?
8 *watch* _____ television *lately*?

I/We	have	eaten some chocolate	today.
			this week.
He/She	has	not eaten any chocolate	recently.
			in the past year.

B Now write about yourself and your friend, using the information you gave each other.

9 I _____
10 He/She _____
11 We _____
12 _____

3.6 Past simple: Pronunciation of regular -ed

Write out the regular past simple forms of the following verbs, putting them into three columns according to their pronunciation.

add   agree   ask   belong   breathe   camp   carry   compete   decide   describe   drop   end   fail
finish   guess   hate   hope   invite   knock   live   miss   open   pass   start   taste   visit   walk

/t/	/d/	/id/
asked	agreed	added

19

VERBS: TIME AND TENSE

3.7 *Since, for, ago: Games*

Past	The ancient Greeks *organized* the first Olympic Games about *3000 years ago*.
Present perfect	We *have held* the modern games *since 1896*. We *have held* them regularly *for the past ninety years*.

Complete the following with *ago*, *for* or *since*.

Football. A game something like football was played over 2000 years ¹_____ in China. The game has certainly been played in England ²_____ hundreds of years. The Football Association was formed over a hundred years ³_____, in 1863. The game has been played with eleven players a side ⁴_____ 1870.

Netball has been played ⁵_____ nearly a hundred years. Actually it has been played ⁶_____ 1891.

Polo has been played ⁷_____ hundreds of years. Some people say that it was first played over 2000 years ⁸_____ in Iran. Others say that it has been played ⁹_____ about A.D. 250, when it was popular in China.

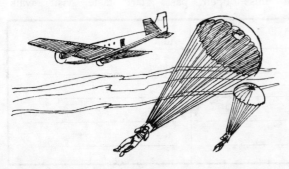

Parachuting became an official sport less than forty years ¹⁰_____ in 1951. Women have only competed ¹¹_____ 1956 – that is ¹²_____ about twenty years.

SECTION 4 AUXILIARIES AND MODALS

4.1 Future opportunity: *can*

If the weather is nice tomorrow, we		go to the pool.
If Suleiman is at the party next Saturday, you		telephone you on Saturday evening.
If you give me your number, I	can	have a picnic.
If you come to England next year, you		send you a postcard.
If you bring your swimming things, we		visit us in Cambridge.
If you give me your address, I		practise your Arabic.

A We can use *can* (or *will be able to*) for future opportunity. Make six sensible sentences from the table, using *can*.

1 _____
2 _____
3 _____
4 _____
5 _____
6 _____

I *can* sit the exam next month, if I want to.	**Opportunity**
You *will be able to* pass the exam when you've studied for another year.	**Future ability**

B *Can* or *will be able to*? Complete the following using *can* if possible. Use *will be able to* where the meaning is future ability, not simple opportunity.

7 I can't understand physics, but I _____ when I'm older.

8 We've missed the 7.30 train, but we _____ get the 8 o'clock if we hurry.

9 We can't afford to go to Spain this year, but we _____ go next year.

10 People can't live on the moon, but perhaps they _____ in the 21st century.

11 I _____ leave school when I'm sixteen.

12 Do you think that at some future date people _____ live under the sea?

13 Perhaps soon they _____ cure cancer.

21

AUXILIARIES AND MODALS

4.2 Past ability: *Two daring people*

General past ability

They *could* do amazing stunts.   ANY TIME
They *could* see she was in danger.   + SEE/HEAR: ONCE OR ANY TIME
The police *couldn't* stop him.   INABILITY: ONCE OR ANY TIME

Success on definite occasion(s)

He *managed to* get out of the box.
She *was able to* hold on to the train.

A Complete the following, using *could*, *couldn't* or *was able to*.

HOUDINI (1874–1926) was the greatest 'escaper' of all time. He ¹_____ get free from all sorts of impossible ropes and chains. He ²_____ also hold his breath under water for a very long time. In one of his favourite tricks he asked people to tie him up and throw him into a river. Of course he ³_____ escape every time. Once he jumped, tied and chained, into a hole in the frozen Detroit River in the USA. And this time he ⁴_____ free himself before the river pulled him under the ice. Everybody thought that this was the end of Houdini. But no. Somehow he ⁵_____ undo the ropes and find the hole in the ice again.

Perhaps his most famous stunt (or trick) was his escape from inside a wooden box, thrown into New York Harbour by some newspaper reporters. The police told Houdini not to jump, but they ⁶_____ stop Houdini. He hired a boat and so he ⁷_____ do the stunt in the middle of the Harbour. The reporters tied up Houdini's hands and feet, and then, when he was in the box, they nailed on the lid and put more chains round the box. They did not know that Houdini ⁸_____ easily open the box because one side had special screws. The box was dropped from the boat, and for nearly a minute everyone waited. Would it be a disaster or success?

Once again Houdini ⁹_____ do the impossible. He came up smiling, and the papers had another marvellous story.

22

AUXILIARIES AND MODALS

B Complete the following using *could, couldn't* or *managed to*.

HELEN GIBSON. There was very little trick photography in the early days of silent films. So the film directors ¹⁰_____ make exciting films unless the film stars ¹¹_____ do stunts. Helen Gibson was an amazing American stunt star. On one occasion she actually ¹²_____ ride a motorbike through the open doors of a train, in at one side and out at the other. She ¹³_____ jump from one moving train to another, and she ¹⁴_____ jump from high buildings. Once she ¹⁵_____ jump from a high tower, and another time she jumped from a station roof. This was the most dangerous stunt she ever did. She ¹⁶_____ land on the moving train, but the train was rolling from side to side. The camera men ¹⁷_____ see she was in great danger but they ¹⁸_____ do anything to help. But fortunately she ¹⁹_____ hold on to the edge of the roof. Once again Helen Gibson was safe.

AUXILIARIES AND MODALS

4.3 Requests and invitations: *could* and *would*

Requests	
Could Would	you help me, please?

Agreeing to a request	
Yes,	of course. certainly.

Refusing a request		
(No,) Oh,	I'm	afraid I can't. sorry. I can't.

A Some of your friends want you to do various things. They ask politely using *Could you . . .?* or *Would you . . .?* You agree to some of the requests and refuse others. Complete the dialogues as indicated.

1 (A friend wants you to lend him your dictionary. You agree.)

YOUR FRIEND Could _____

YOU _____

2 (He wants you to do his English homework for him. You refuse.)

YOUR FRIEND Would _____

YOU _____

3 (Another friend wants you to turn down your radio. You agree.)

YOUR FRIEND Could _____

YOU _____

4 (She also wants you to look after her pet snake. You refuse.)

YOUR FRIEND Would _____

YOU _____

Invitations	
Could you Would you like to	come to the pictures?

Accepting an invitation
Oh thanks. I'd love to.

Refusing an invitation
I'm sorry. I'd love to, but I can't.

B Complete the dialogues as indicated.

5 (You invite a friend to come to the football match with you tomorrow. The friend accepts.)

YOU Could _____

YOUR FRIEND _____

24

AUXILIARIES AND MODALS

6 (You invite another friend to go to the *Police* concert next week. She refuses.)

YOU Could _____

YOUR FRIEND _____

7 (You invite a friend to come and meet your parents. He accepts.)

YOU Would _____

YOUR FRIEND _____

8 (You invite this friend to play chess with you. He refuses.)

YOU Would _____

YOUR FRIEND _____

4.4 Advice: *What had he better do?*

▲ What had I better do?

● Hadn't you better see your doctor?
You had better stop eating so much.
You'd better not eat those chocolates.

A This man is overweight and unhealthy. He'll die young if he isn't careful! He asks his friends for advice. Rewrite what they all say, using *had better (not)* – or question forms – instead of the words in *italics*.

1 You *should* eat less. <u>You had better eat less.</u>

2 You *ought to* eat more vegetables. _____

3 You *shouldn't* drink so many fizzy drinks. _____

4 You *ought not to* take sugar in your tea. _____

5 *Shouldn't* you take more exercise? _____

6 You *should not* watch so much television. _____

7 You *oughtn't to* eat so much salt. _____

8 *Oughtn't* you *to* go to the dentist? _____

B Are they right? What is your advice for this man?

9 He had better _____

10 He'd better not _____

C And what had you yourself better do if you want to be healthier?

11 I'd better _____

12 I had better not _____

AUXILIARIES AND MODALS

4.5 Have you got ...? Do you have ...? Are you having ...?

Have you (got) a pain?	Yes, I have.
Stephan has (got) two sisters, hasn't he?	Yes, he has.
Do you (usually) have classes on Wednesdays?	Yes, we do.
Are they having a lesson now?	Yes, they are.

Complete the following with a suitable form of have. (There are alternatives in some cases.) Use question forms and negatives as necessary and as indicated. Remember to make question tags and short answers agree with the questions.

▲ What's the matter?
■ ¹I _____ flu, I think.
▲ And ² _____ you _____ a headache too?
■ Yes, I ³ _____.
▲ ⁴ _____ you often _____ headaches?
■ No, I ⁵ _____.

■ Hello. Am I interrupting you?
▲ Well, I ⁶ (just) _____ dinner actually.
■ You ⁷ _____ n't usually _____ dinner so early, ⁸ _____ you?
▲ No, I ⁹ _____. But I ¹⁰ _____ a lot of work to do before bedtime.
■ Oh, dear, ¹¹ _____ you?

■ ¹² _____ you _____ a bath or shower in this house?
▲ We ¹³ _____ a bath actually.
■ Mm. Tom's been a long time in there now. ¹⁴ _____ he _____ a bath?

■ ¹⁵ I _____ second thoughts about taking the exam.
▲ ¹⁶ _____ you? You mustn't. You ¹⁷ _____ a very good chance of passing.
■ ¹⁸ _____ I?

■ We ¹⁹ _____ a barbecue lunch tomorrow. Would you like to come?
▲ Oh dear. I'm taking Rachel to the dentist. She ²⁰ _____ an appointment at 12.30.
■ Oh, what a pity. ²¹ _____ she _____ toothache?
▲ No, she ²² _____ a check-up. That's all. She ²³ _____ one every year.

4.6 What will he be doing?

> ▲ What *will* he *be doing* this time next week?
> ■ He*'ll be taking* his intermediate class.
> ▲ *Will* he *be taking* them next Wednesday morning?
> ■ Yes, he *will* (be).
> ▲ And in the afternoon?
> ■ No, he *won't* (be). He *won't be teaching* them then.

Here is David Green's timetable for this term. It is 9.30 a.m. on Tuesday 9th March. David is taking his intermediate class.

	MONDAY	TUESDAY	WEDNESDAY	THURSDAY	FRIDAY
9.00-10.00	Intermediate	Intermediate	Intermediate	Intermediate	Intermediate
10.00-10.45	Intermediate	Intermediate	Intermediate	Intermediate	Intermediate
10.45-11.05	COFFEE BREAK					
11.05-12.00	Advanced		Advanced		
12.00-1.00	Advanced		Advanced		
1.00-2.00		staff meeting	LUNCH		
2.00-3.00		Beginners	17th cancelled	Beginners	Beginners
3.00-4.00	Translation	Beginners	Literature	Beginners	

Complete the dialogue in the *will be DOING* tense, using information from the timetable and a suitable verb. Use the verbs *do, attend* (a staff meeting), *have* (lunch), *take* (his _____ class), *work* (in the staffroom). You can give short answers in two places.

■ What will David Green be doing before break next Wednesday?

▲ He ¹ _will be taking his intermediate class._

■ ² _____ the same class after the coffee break too?

▲ No, he ³ _____. He ⁴ _____ then.

■ And what ⁵ _____ at 1.15 on Monday?

▲ Oh, that's lunch time. I suppose ⁶ _____

■ ⁷ _____ lunch at that time every day next week?

▲ Yes, he ⁸ _____, except on Tuesday, when he ⁹ _____

■ Well, when can I telephone him? What about 3 o'clock next Thursday?

▲ Oh, not Thursday. He ¹⁰ _____ then. But Wednesday is possible. He ¹¹ _____ that afternoon, because Miss White has organized a theatre visit. I expect Mr Green ¹² _____ in the staffroom then. That would be a good time to call him.

AUXILIARIES AND MODALS

4.7 Will DO or will be DOING: In the travel agent's

will DO	Come on. You*'ll enjoy* it. You *won't want* to come back. } PREDICTION *Will* you *send* me a postcard? REQUEST Of course we *will*. PROMISE/DECISION NOW
will be DOING	What *will* they *be doing* this time next week? } FUTURE ACTIVITY They*'ll be lying* on the beach. IN PROGRESS

Marie-Christine has arranged a holiday in Italy for two of her friends. Here they all are in the travel agent's. Complete the conversation with *will DO* or *will be DOING*, using the verbs given, and negatives (with *won't*) if necessary.

MARIE-CHRISTINE When you arrive in Rome, the guide (¹ wait) _will be waiting_ for you.

PIERRE But how (² recognize) _will we recognize_ her? I mean, we (³ know) _____ her. Perhaps we (⁴ see) _____ her.

MARIE-CHRISTINE Oh, she (⁵ wear) _____ a badge. Anyway she (⁶ find) _____ you. Don't worry. You (⁷ miss) _____ her.

GENEVIEVE Oh dear. This time on Thursday we (⁸ sit) _____ in a hot sticky coach. I don't think I want to do all that sightseeing.

PIERRE Oh come on. You (⁹ enjoy) _____ it. Anyway, this time next week, we (¹⁰ lie) _____ in the sun at Amalfi getting brown.

MARIE-CHRISTINE And this time tomorrow, you (¹¹ fly) _____ over the Alps having lunch. Lucky you. Genevieve, (¹² you do) _____ something for me? (¹³ you bring) _____ me back a leather handbag? I (¹⁴ pay) _____ for it of course.

GENEVIEVE Of course. We (¹⁵ bring) _____ you two bags if you like. But we (¹⁶ allow) _____ you to pay. No way!

MARIE-CHRISTINE I'm sorry I can't come to the airport tomorrow, but I (¹⁷ work) _____ then. By the way, you (¹⁸ remember) _____ your passports, won't you?

AUXILIARIES AND MODALS

GENEVIEVE Oh dear. What ([19] happen) _____ if we lose our passports?

MARIE-CHRISTINE You ([20] lose) _____ your passports. Don't be silly. Enjoy yourselves.

SECTION 5 ADJECTIVES AND ADVERBS

5.1 Some adjectives and adverbs: The same word or different?

Adjective & adverb = different		
Irregular	good	well
Regular	bad	badly
	clever	cleverly
	easy	easily
	quick	quickly
	slow	slowly
	sudden	suddenly

Adjective & adverb = same	
early	last
fast	late
first	long
hard	low
high	

Complete the following with the right adverb corresponding to the adjectives given.

■ Is the *first* letter in the alphabet A and the *last* Z?

▲ That's right. Z comes ¹ *last* and A comes ² *first*.

● You're always *late*. Please try to be *early* tomorrow.
▲ That's not fair. I don't usually arrive ³_____. I got here ⁴_____ yesterday. I haven't got a *bad* record. I don't do too ⁵_____. I'm sorry, but it's not my fault if the bus was *slow*. All the traffic was moving ⁶_____. Anyway, you haven't been waiting ⁷_____, have you?
● Yes, I've been waiting a very *long* time. You could ⁸_____ get here on time. It's quite *easy* if you try. It's not *hard*. You just don't try ⁹_____ enough.

▲ What is *fast* food?
■ It means food that you can eat ¹⁰_____ – perhaps standing up in a cheap restaurant. It's also prepared very ¹¹_____.
▲ Who wants a *quick* meal?
■ Well I agree really. But actually the food is *good* here. And they serve it very ¹²_____.

We could hear a plane *high* above the clouds. It was flying very very ¹³_____. Then we had a *sudden* sight of it through the clouds, and it was ¹⁴_____ flying ¹⁵_____ over our heads. It was very *low* – I thought it was going to crash. But the pilot was obviously very *clever* and he ¹⁶_____ flew up again and away.

30

ANSWERS

1.1 POSSESSIVES: *MY, MINE*

1 yours 2 mine 3 my 4 hers 5 his 6 his
7 your 8 mine 9 my 10 your 11 ours 12 our
13 their 14 Theirs 15 her 16 her

1.2 *A FRIEND OF MINE*

1 of his 2 of hers 3 of theirs 4 of ours 5 of mine
6 of yours

1.3 *AN APPLE A DAY*

A 1 once a month 2 US$ 850 an ounce 3 54.4 hours a week 4 70 miles an hour 5 233 pounds of potatoes a year 6 32.3 hours a week 7 a mile a minute 8 twice a day 9 1000 miles an hour 10 5 million barrels of oil a day.

1.4 *SOME* OR *ANY: A TRICK WITH PAPER*

2 some 3 any 4 some 5 some 6 any/some
7 any 8 some 9 some 10 Any 11 some 12 any
13 any 14 some 15 any 16 some 17 some
18 Any

1.5 *ANYTHING, EVERYONE, SOMEBODY, NOWHERE*

A 2 anything 3 nothing 4 Everything 5 Everyone
6 Someone 7 no one 8 Anyone 9 anywhere
10 somewhere 11 everywhere 12 nowhere
B 13 everyone/everybody 14 everyone/everybody
15 nothing 16 nowhere 17 something 18 anywhere
19 something 20 anyone/anybody

1.6 *MUCH, MANY, A LOT: A HOLIDAY IN PORTUGAL*

1 many ... are there 2 aren't many 3 many ... are there 4 are a lot of 5 much ... is there 6 isn't much
7 are a lot of 8 much ... is there 9 many ... are there
10 much ... is there 11 is a lot of 12 isn't much

1.7 *A FEW, A LITTLE, VERY FEW, VERY LITTLE*

3 There is very little toothpaste. 4 There are a few paper handkerchiefs. 5 There is very little sun oil. 6 There is a little soap. 7 There are a few sweets. 8 There are very few films.

2.1 MASS OR COUNT NOUNS: *IN HOSPITAL* OR *IN A HOSPITAL?*

1 Ø 2 Ø 3 a 4 Ø 5 Ø 6 a 7 Ø 8 Ø 9 the
10 a/the 11 Ø 12 Ø 13 the 14 the 15 the
16 Ø 17 the 18 Ø 19 Ø 20 the 21 Ø 22 Ø
23 a 24 Ø 25 a

2.2 PLURALS: *FASCINATING FACTS*

2 cliffs 3 Hovercraft 4 policewomen 5 sheep ... Sheep 6 geese 7 potatoes 8 brothers-in-law
9 loaves 10 Cod ... fish 11 pence ... pennies
12 handkerchiefs 13 spacemen 14 volcanoes
15 shelves 16 kangaroos ... zoos 17 lay-bys
18 hooves ... roofs 19 take-aways 20 lives ... crises

2.3 SINGULAR OR PLURAL?

1 have 2 say 3 are 4 is 5 some 6 pairs of glasses 7 is 8 Were 9 some 10 are

3.1 PRESENT PROGRESSIVE: *WHAT ARE THEY ALL DOING?*

2 is skiing ... is working 3 is watching TV ... is calling 4 is having breakfast ... is having lunch 5 is studying ... is also studying 6 are shopping ... is sleeping

3.2 PRESENT PROGRESSIVE: *ARE YOU DOING ANYTHING NEXT WEEK?*

2 are going to the school concert 3 are having dinner with Bob's mother 4 am meeting 5 are seeing 'A Passage to India' 6 am having lunch 7 am going to the hairdresser's 8 am meeting Tom at Heathrow
9 am taking Rachel and Andrew to the dentist 10 aren't doing

3.3 ASKING QUESTIONS: *JOGGING*

2 How did he become a millionaire? 3 What happened to him? 4 What was he doing when he died? 5 Did people immediately stop jogging? 6 How much do some people jog? 7 And when do most people jog?
8 Doesn't regular exercise do the heart good? 9 Does jogging actually ever cause heart attacks? 10 And what sort of evidence is emerging now to prove that jogging is good for you? 11 Who wants to die young?

3.4 PRESENT PERFECT: *BEEN, COME* OR *GONE?*

2 have ... gone 3 has ... gone 4 has been 5 has ... gone 6 has ... been 7 has come 8 has gone
9 hasn't gone 10 has been 11 has ... been 12 has come 13 have gone 14 has been 15 has gone

3.5 PRESENT PERFECT: *HAVE YOU READ ANY GOOD BOOKS LATELY?*

A 2 Have you eaten 3 Have you been 4 Have you read 5 Have you bought 6 Have you been 7 Have you grown out of 8 Have you watched

3.6 PAST SIMPLE: PRONUNCIATION OF REGULAR –ED

/t/ asked camped dropped finished guessed hoped knocked missed passed walked
/d/ agreed belonged breathed carried described failed lived opened
/ɪd/ added competed decided ended hated invited started tasted visited

3.7 SINCE, FOR, AGO: GAMES

1 ago   2 for   3 ago   4 since   5 for   6 since   7 for   8 ago   9 since   10 ago   11 since   12 for

4.1 FUTURE OPPORTUNITY: *CAN*

A 1 If the weather is nice tomorrow, we can have a picnic.   2 If Suleiman is at the party next Saturday, you can practise your Arabic.   3 If you give me your number, I can telephone you on Saturday evening.   4 If you come to England next year, you can visit us in Cambridge.   5 If you bring your swimming things, we can go to the pool.   6 If you give me your address, I can send you a postcard.
B 7 will be able to   8 can   9 will be able to   10 will be able to   11 can   12 will be able to   13 will be able to

4.2 PAST ABILITY: *TWO DARING PEOPLE*

A 1 could   2 could   3 was able to   4 couldn't   5 was able to   6 couldn't   7 was able to   8 could   9 was able to
B 10 couldn't   11 could   12 managed to   13 could   14 could   15 managed to   16 managed to   17 could   18 couldn't   19 managed to

4.3 REQUESTS AND INVITATIONS: *COULD* AND *WOULD*

A 1 Could you lend me your dictionary, please? (Yes of course/Yes certainly.)   2 Would you do my English homework for me, please? (I'm afraid/I'm sorry I can't.)   3 Could you turn down your transistor radio, please? (Yes of course/Yes certainly.)   4 Would you look after my pet snake, please? (I'm afraid/I'm sorry I can't.)
B 5 Could you come to the football match with me tomorrow? (Oh thanks. I'd love to.)   6 Could you come to the *Police* concert next week? (I'm sorry. I'd love to, but I can't.)   7 Would you like to come and meet my parents? (Oh thanks. I'd love to.)   8 Would you like to play chess with me? (I'm sorry. I'd love to, but I can't.)

4.4 ADVICE: *WHAT HAD HE BETTER DO?*

A 2 You had better eat . . .   3 You had better not drink . . .   4 You had better not take . . .   5 Hadn't you better take . . .   6 You had better not watch . . .   7 You had better not eat . . .   8 Hadn't you better go . . .

4.5 *HAVE YOU GOT . . . ? DO YOU HAVE . . . ? ARE YOU HAVING . . . ?*

1 have (got)   2 have you got   3 have   4 Do you often have   5 don't   6 am just having   7 don't usually have   8 do you   9 don't   10 have (got)   11 have   12 Have you got/Do you have   13 have (got)   14 Is he having   15 am having   16 Are   17 have + 18 Have/Do (OR 17 have got + 18 Have)   19 are having   20 has (got)   21 Has she got   22 is having   23 has

4.6 WHAT WILL HE BE DOING?

2 Will he be taking   3 won't (be)   4 will be taking his advanced class   5 will he be doing   6 he'll be having lunch   7 Will he be having   8 will (be)   9 will be attending a staff meeting   10 will be taking his beginners' class   11 won't be taking his literature class   12 will be working

4.7 *WILL DO* OR *WILL BE DOING*: IN THE TRAVEL AGENT'S

3 won't know   4 won't see   5 will be wearing   6 will find   7 won't miss   8 will be sitting   9 will enjoy   10 will be lying   11 will be flying   12 will you do   13 Will you bring   14 will pay   15 will bring   16 won't allow   17 will be working   18 will remember   19 will happen   20 won't lose

5.1 SOME ADJECTIVES AND ADVERBS: THE SAME WORD OR DIFFERENT?

3 late   4 early   5 badly   6 slowly   7 long   8 easily   9 hard   10 fast   11 quickly   12 well   13 high   14 suddenly   15 low   16 cleverly

5.2 COMPARISON OF ADJECTIVES: *THE SINCLAIR C5*

A 1 more convenient   2 simpler to drive   3 cheaper   4 easier to park   5 more economical   6 more practical   7 quieter   8 more enjoyable   9 more exciting   10 more modern

5.3 COMPARATIVES AND SUPERLATIVES: *SOME WORLD RECORDS*

1 highest . . . in . . . highest . . . in . . . the . . . of   2 large . . . larger than . . . larger . . . of . . . largest . . . in . . . largest   3 the . . . in . . . longer than . . . longest . . . in . . . longer than longest . . . in   4 taller than . . . tallest . . . in . . . taller . . . taller than . . . tallest of . . . tallest . . . in   5 high . . . higher than . . . higher than . . . of . . . highest   6 remote . . . remoter/more remote than . . . remotest/most remote . . . in . . . of . . . remotest/most remote   7 smaller . . . smaller than . . . smallest of   8 the . . . bigger than . . . bigger than . . . of . . . biggest . . . in

5.4 POSITION OF TIME ADVERBIALS: OFTEN? EVERY DAY?

A 1 I never go to the cinema on Fridays. 2 Tom often goes swimming at the weekend. 3 We usually watch television in the evening. 4 She walks here three times a week. 5 He rarely stays up late on weekdays. 6 She never goes jogging in the evening.

5.5 ENOUGH MONEY, YOUNG ENOUGH: HANG-GLIDING

2 And I don't have enough time. 3 Or perhaps I am not interested enough. 4 Stephan says that hang-gliding is safe enough. 5 But you must have enough warm air. 6 I haven't enough courage to jump off a cliff. 7 I am not brave enough to try. 8 And I am not patient enough to learn.

6.1 SOME PREPOSITIONS OF PLACE: THE TRANS-SIBERIAN RAILWAY

1 across 2 from 3 in 4 to 5 in 6 for 7 Between 8 through 9 at 10 past/through 11 Beyond 12 along 13 towards 14 to 15 from 16 to 17 via

6.2 OVER AND ABOVE

2 over his head 3 over the river 4 above sea level 5 over his eye 6 over the wall 7 above his eye 8 over Rachel 9 above/over the bed 10 above us 11 above the bank 12 over his shirt

6.3 UNDER AND BELOW

1 under the cloth 2 under the table 3 below sea level 4 under the river 5 below zero 6 under (the) water 7 below them 8 under the trees 9 under the tap 10 below the post office 11 below the village 12 under her head

6.4 A TRICK: THE PIN IN THE BOTTLE

1 with 2 into 3 out of 4 without 5 from 6 behind 7 for 8 Before 9 in 10 of 11 up 12 of 13 out of 14 without 15 of

6.5 AN ACROSTIC: OPPOSITES

1 into 2 off 3 down 4 above 5 from 6 under 7 against 8 towards 9 away from

7.1 DOWN, OFF, ON, OUT

1 touched down 2 broken down 3 go on 4 going off 5 turn ... off 6 put ... on 7 go out 8 worn out 9 sit down 10 puts ... off

7.2 UP: ANDREW AND RACHEL

1 woken up 2 sitting up 3 get up 4 broke up 5 winding up 6 grown up 7 putting up 8 blowing up

7.3 PREPOSITIONAL VERBS: THE SUITCASE

1 looking at 2 belongs to 3 listening to 4 occur to 5 hoping for 6 laughing at 7 waiting for 8 send for 9 looking for 10 look after

8.1 VERBS OF PERCEPTION: I SAW HIM RUN/RUNNING

3 him running 4 him looking through the windows 5 somebody scream 6 something burning 7 smoke pouring out of the house 8 this other man coming up behind me 9 him suddenly touch me 10 him putting a cloth over my eyes 11 the fire engine arrive 12 him running away very fast

8.2 AGREE TO DO, CONSIDER DOING

1 to win 2 to break 3 feeling 4 being 5 to overcome 6 to be 7 being 8 turning 9 being 10 to practise 11 to help 12 to advertise 13 to do 14 skating 15 to be 16 practising 17 worrying 18 worrying

8.3 LET, MAKE: WHAT DO THE NOTICES MEAN?

2 They don't let you walk on the grass. 3 They don't let you pick the flowers. 4 They make you drive on the left. 5 They let you park free. 6 They don't let you cycle in the park. 7 They make you pay £1 to enter. 8 They let you bring children in. 9 They don't let you pay by cheque. 10 They make you sit at the back of the bus if you smoke.

8.4 INDIRECT OBJECTS: TO OR FOR?

2 he chose some for 3 I gave it to 4 he kept one for 5 she lent it to 6 I passed it to 7 I found one for 8 I promised one to 9 I sent one to 10 she made one for 11 I saved some for 12 I owed some to

8.5 INFINITIVES: CAREERS

A 1 to ask 2 to pass 3 to improve 4 to continue 5 to do 6 to get 7 to apply 8 to talk 9 to see 10 to work
B 11 To be a teacher 12 To succeed in banking 13 To work in a travel agency 14 To become a ski instructor 15 To be a good writer

9.1 TRUE CONDITIONS: *SNAKES AND LADDERS*

A 3 land . . . go down   4 land . . . stay   5 land
6 throw . . . land . . . go down   7 throw . . . land . . . go up
8 throw . . . land . . . stay   9 throw . . . land . . . stay
10 throw . . . land . . . go down
Answer 43
B 11 e   12 d   13 f   14 a   15 b   16 c

9.2 CONDITIONS: *FUTURE POSSIBILITIES*

2a If I have enough money, I'll buy . . .   2b If I haven't (got)/don't have . . . I won't buy one.   3a If I eat too much, I'll get fat.   3b If I don't eat . . . I'll stay slim.
4a If I pass my exams . . . I'll go up . . .   4b If I don't pass, I'll have to take them again.   5a If I win a prize, I'll be delighted.   5b If I don't win, I won't be surprised!
6a If I telephone . . . I'll tell her . . .   6b If I don't telephone . . . I'll have to write . . .   7a If I work harder, my parents will be pleased.   7b If I don't work harder, they'll be cross.

9.3 CONDITIONS: *IF ONLY THINGS WERE DIFFERENT NOW!*

A 2 If I were a princess, I would live in a palace.   3 If I had (got) wings, I could fly away like a bird.   4 If I didn't have to come to school, I would be free.   5 If I could play tennis well, I could be a world champion.   6 If the work weren't/wasn't so difficult, I wouldn't have to spend so much time on it.   7 If we lived in a really hot country, we would go swimming every day.   8 If I really understood French, I could do it.

9.4 WISHING: *SHE WISHES THINGS WERE DIFFERENT NOW*

A 2 She wishes she had (got) wings.   3 She wishes she were free.   4 She wishes she could play . . .   5 She wishes the work weren't/wasn't . . .   6 She wishes she and Andrew lived . . .   7 She wishes they went swimming . . .   8 She wishes she didn't have to spend . . .

9.5 WISHING ABOUT THE FUTURE: *THINGS COULD BE DIFFERENT ONE DAY*

A 1 I wish I could buy . . .   2 I wish I could go . . .
3 But I wish I could learn.   4 We wish we could leave . . .   5 I wish I could become . . .
B 6 tidy   7 I wish you two would hurry   8 I wish he would telephone   9 I wish you could come   10 he couldn't see

9.6 MORE RELATIVE CLAUSES

2 What was that film about a shark that terrorized people for years?   3 What was the name of that actress who became Princess Grace of Monaco?   4 Star Wars is a film you really must see.   5 'Beverly Hills Cop' and 'Trading Places' were two Eddie Murphy films that amused me very much.   6 The Beatles were four young men from Liverpool who became world-famous.   7 Liverpool is a city in northern England most tourists never visited.
8 But now there are guided tours you can take round Liverpool.   9 Elvis Presley was a great pop star everyone has heard of.   10 Joan Armatrading is a singer people admire today.   11 I've got lots of cassettes that remind me of my favourite films.   12 Barbra Streisand is an actress I'm sure you've seen.

9.7 RELATIVE CLAUSES WITH PREPOSITIONS AT THE END

2 something you can sit on or lean against.   3 thing you fasten papers together with.   4 thing you can open tins with.   5 something swimmers and divers jump off.
6 something you pour liquids from.   7 bag you can keep money in.   8 something you climb up and down.   9 a 'box' people spend too long looking at.

9.8 RELATIVE CLAUSES: *WHO, WHICH, WHOSE*

2 This is an aunt of mine whose family have lived there for 300 years.   3 These are some friends whose farm I've often stayed on.   4 This is a part of Poland which has a very good climate.   5 These are some people who were staying there last year.   6 This is a city which always interests visitors.   7 This is a hotel which is very good value.   8 This is the aunt who gave me my cassette player.   9 This is a friend who is coming to visit me soon.
10 This is a church which has lovely windows.

9.9 WHAT TO DO: *A CRASH SURVIVOR*

1 where to look   2 what to do   3 where to look for one
4 which way to go   5 how to make a simple raft
6 when to sleep   7 how to get them out   8 what to eat
9 which plants to eat   10 which to avoid

ADJECTIVES AND ADVERBS

5.2 Comparison of adjectives: *The Sinclair C5*

The C5 is	more exciting	than	a car.
	better		a bicycle.
	nicer		

A Here is the Sinclair C5 – a three-wheel electric vehicle, which first appeared in 1985. The makers claimed that it was:

1 convenient
2 simple to drive
3 cheap
4 easy to park
5 economical
6 practical
7 quiet
8 enjoyable
9 exciting
10 modern

Complete the table, saying how – according to the makers – the C5 compared with a car.

They said the C5 was

1 _____
2 _____
3 _____
4 _____
5 _____
6 _____ than a car.
7 _____
8 _____
9 _____
10 _____

31

ADJECTIVES AND ADVERBS

I think the C5 would be	more less	comfortable conspicuous controllable dangerous difficult to drive exciting expensive powerful	than	a bicycle. a car. a motorbike.

B *What do you think?* Do you think the C5 would be *more* or *less* comfortable than a bicycle? a car? a motorbike? Use the table to write 8 sentences giving some of your opinions.

11 _____
12 _____
13 _____
14 _____
15 _____
16 _____
17 _____
18 _____

I think I don't think	bicycles motorbikes cars buses trains helicopters planes	are as	safe dangerous comfortable pleasant noisy fast	as	bicycles. motorbikes. cars. buses. trains. helicopters. planes.

C *What do you think about travelling generally?* Use the table to make sensible sentences, saying what you think.

19 _____
20 _____
21 _____
22 _____
23 _____
24 _____
25 _____
26 _____

ADJECTIVES AND ADVERBS

5.3 Comparatives and superlatives: *Some world records*

| high | higher than ... | the highest in/of ... |

Complete the following, using the information given. The answers are at the bottom of the next page.

1 *High mountains*

Aconcagua is the _highest_ mountain _in_ South America. It is _higher_ _than_ Kilimanjaro, which is the _____ mountain _____ Africa. The _____ mountain _____ Asia is Everest. Which is _____ highest _____ the three?

Aconcagua	7035 m
Everest	?
Kilimanjaro	5888 m

Answer: _____

2 *Large islands*

Iceland is a _____ island. But Sumatra is _____ _____ Iceland, and Malagasy is even _____. But none _____ these is the _____ island _____ the world. Can you name the world's _____ island?

Iceland	102,973 sq km
Malagasy	594,180 sq km
Sumatra	431,984 sq km

Answer: _____

3 *Long Rivers*

The Amazon is _____ longest river _____ South America. It is _____ _____ the Yangtze-kiang, which is the _____ river _____ China. But the Nile is even _____ _____ the Amazon. Which is the _____ river _____ the world?

Amazon	6448 km
Nile	?
Yangtze-kiang	5374 km

Answer: _____

4 *Tall Office Buildings*

The National Westminster Bank is _____ _____ any other building in London, and is the _____ building _____ Britain. But the Sears Tower, Chicago, is _____, and so is the Sunshine 6 Building in Tokyo. Is the Sunshine 6 Building _____ _____ the Sears Tower or not? Which is the _____ _____ the three? Which is the _____ office building _____ the world?

National Westminster Bank, London	183 m
Sears Tower, Chicago	443 m
Sunshine 6 Building, Tokyo	?

Answer: _____

33

ADJECTIVES AND ADVERBS

5 *High cities*

Three South American countries have their most important cities _____ in the Andes. Quito is _____ _____ Bogota, and La Paz is also _____ _____ Bogota. Which _____ these three cities is the _____?

Bogota (Colombia)	2610 m
La Paz (Bolivia)	?
Quito (Ecuador)	3225 m

Answer: _____

6 *Remote islands*

Bouvet, St Helena and Tristan da Cunha are all _____ islands in the Atlantic Ocean. Tristan da Cunha is _____ _____ St Helena, and Bouvet is the _____ island _____ the world. Do you know which _____ these three is the _____ inhabited island?

Bouvet Island
St Helena
Tristan da Cunha

Answer: _____

7 *Small States*

Europe contains four very small states. Liechtenstein is _____ than Andorra, and San Marino is _____ _____ Liechtenstein. Which is the _____ _____ them all?

Andorra	492 sq km
Liechtenstein	161 sq km
Monaco	?
San Marino	60 sq km

Answer: _____

8 *Big Deserts*

The Gobi Desert is _____ biggest desert in Asia. It is _____ _____ the Rub Al Khali in Saudi Arabia. But the Sahara is _____ _____ the Gobi. So which _____ these three is the _____ desert _____ the world?

Gobi	1,554,000 sq km
Rub al Khali	?
Sahara	9,065,000 sq km

Answer: _____

Answers: **1** Everest (8848 m) **2** Greenland **3** The Nile (6670 m) **4** The Sears Tower (The Sunshine 6 Building is 240m) **5** La Paz (3631 m) **6** Tristan da Cunha (nobody lives on Bouvet) **7** Monaco (16 sq km) **8** The Sahara (The Rub al Khali is 777,000 sq km)

ADJECTIVES AND ADVERBS

5.4 Position of time adverbials: *often? every day?*

I		watch television.	
I	often	watch television	most evenings.
We	never	watch television	in the morning.

A Can you rearrange these words into sentences?

1 I Fridays go on cinema never to the

2 swimming the Tom goes often at weekend

3 television usually we watch evening the in

4 she here times walks week a three

5 weekdays late stays rarely he up on

6 evening jogging never goes in she the

a
always
usually
often
sometimes
never

7 come to school/college by car
8 walk here
9 watch television
10 read an English book
11 go swimming
12 go to the cinema

b
every day
most days
once/twice/three times a week
at the weekend
on Wednesdays etc.

B Write some sentences about yourself and your friends, using phrases 7–12 and words from the boxes. Notice where the (a) words and the (b) words go.

7
8
9
10
11
12

35

ADJECTIVES AND ADVERBS

5.5 Enough money, young enough: Hang-gliding

Enough + noun	Have you got *enough* money?
Adjective + enough	You are young *enough* to try.

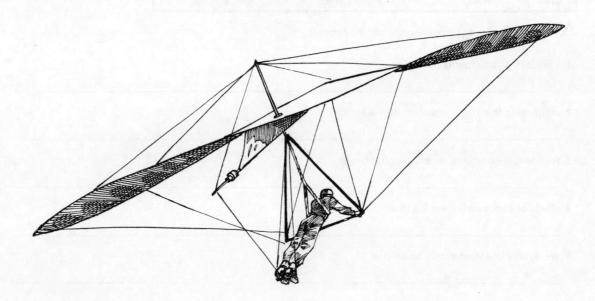

Unscramble the sentences.

1 I money hang-glider buy to a enough haven't

   I *haven't enough money to buy a hang-glider.*

2 I and time have enough don't

   And _____

3 I or perhaps interested not enough am

   Or _____

4 Stephan hang-gliding safe that enough is says

   Stephan _____

5 You but air warm enough have must

   But _____

6 I cliff courage jump to a off enough haven't

   I _____

7 I not brave try to enough am

   I _____

8 And am patient not learn to enough I

   And _____

36

SECTION 6 PREPOSITIONS

6.1 Some prepositions of place: *The Trans-Siberian Railway*

across	in
along	past
at	through
between ... (and) ...	to
beyond	towards
for	via
from ... to ...	

Use the prepositions in the box to complete the following. You may need to use some words more than once. Also note that in some places there is more than one possible answer.

The Trans-Siberian railway runs right ¹_____ the Soviet Union ²_____ Moscow ³_____ the west ⁴_____ Vladivostok ⁵_____ the east. It stretches ⁶_____ thousands of kilometres.

⁷_____ Moscow and Sverdlovsk the train goes ⁸_____ the Ural Mountains. Then it crosses the European-Asian border ⁹_____ Omsk and continues ¹⁰_____ ever-changing scenery on its long journey east.

¹¹_____ Irkutz the line runs ¹²_____ the shores of Lake Baikal before it divides into two. The Trans-Siberian line itself continues ¹³_____ the Pacific Ocean, as far as Khabarovsk and Vladivostok. Another line goes south ¹⁴_____ Ulan Bator, Beijing and eventually Hong Kong.

It is possible to travel overland by train all the way ¹⁵_____ Paris ¹⁶_____ Hong Kong ¹⁷_____ Moscow, Irkutz and Beijing.

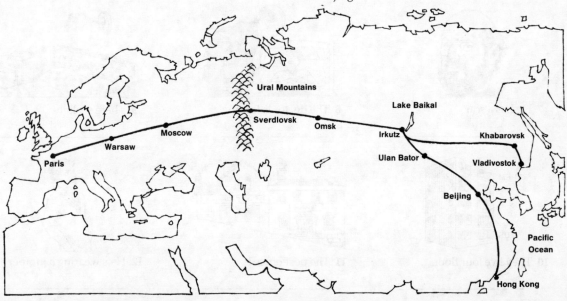

PREPOSITIONS

6.2 *Over* and *above*

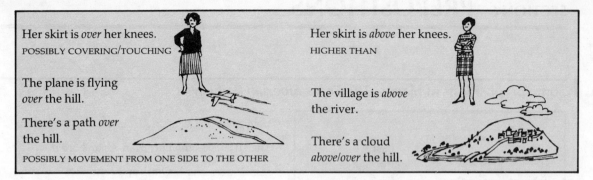

Her skirt is *over* her knees.
POSSIBLY COVERING/TOUCHING

The plane is flying *over* the hill.

There's a path *over* the hill.
POSSIBLY MOVEMENT FROM ONE SIDE TO THE OTHER

Her skirt is *above* her knees.
HIGHER THAN

The village is *above* the river.

There's a cloud *above/over* the hill.

Complete the following, using *over* or *above* and any other words you need to describe the pictures.

1 He's put his coat
over the chair.

2 He's got a cloth

3 There's a bridge

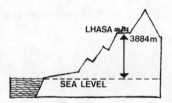

4 Lhasa (in Tibet) is 3884 m

5 He has a patch

6 The cat has jumped

7 He has a scar

8 The doctor is leaning

9 There's a light

10 They live four floors

11 The post office is

12 He's wearing a jumper

6.3 Under and below

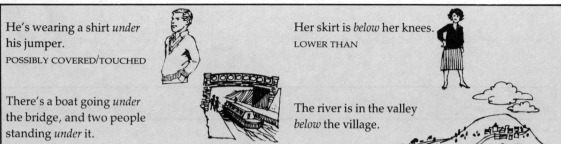

He's wearing a shirt *under* his jumper.
POSSIBLY COVERED/TOUCHED

There's a boat going *under* the bridge, and two people standing *under* it.
POSSIBLY MOVEMENT FROM ONE SIDE TO THE OTHER

Her skirt is *below* her knees.
LOWER THAN

The river is in the valley *below* the village.

Complete the following, using *under* or *below* and any other words you need to describe the pictures.

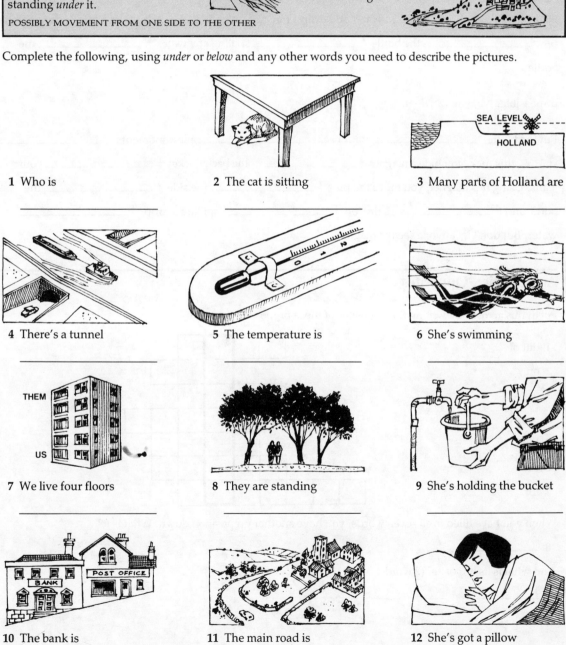

1 Who is

2 The cat is sitting

3 Many parts of Holland are

4 There's a tunnel

5 The temperature is

6 She's swimming

7 We live four floors

8 They are standing

9 She's holding the bucket

10 The bank is

11 The main road is

12 She's got a pillow

PREPOSITIONS

6.4 A trick: *The pin in the bottle*

Use these prepositions to find out how to do this trick.

a bottle of water   a pocket   a magnet

| before | behind | for | from | in | into | of (3) | out of (2) | up | with | without (2) |

Fill a bottle ¹_____ water and drop a pin ²_____ it. Ask your friends to get the pin ³_____ the bottle ⁴_____ spilling any water ⁵_____ the bottle.

Impossible? No, you can do it.

Put the bottle ⁶_____ your back ⁷_____ a few moments. ⁸_____ starting this trick, you hide a magnet ⁹_____ the back pocket ¹⁰_____ your jeans. Using this magnet, you move the pin ¹¹_____ the side ¹²_____ the bottle and ¹³_____ the top ¹⁴_____ spilling a drop ¹⁵_____ water. But don't let anyone see the magnet!

6.5 An acrostic: Opposites

Fill in this acrostic by writing the opposites of these prepositions:

1 out of
2 on
3 up
4 below
5 to
6 over
7 for

When you have filled in all seven words, you have another preposition down. What is it?

8 _____

And what is its opposite? (2 words)

9 _____ _____

SECTION 7 PHRASAL VERBS

7.1 Down, off, on, out

| break
sit
touch | down | go
put (somebody)
turn (something) | off | go
put (something) | on | go
wear | out |

Complete the following, using the phrasal verbs shown. Put them into the correct tense.

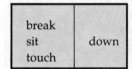

This plane has just ¹_____ safely on the runway.

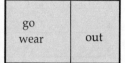

WENDY   You'll be cold if you don't ⁶_____ your jumper _____. It's cold outside.

DAVID   I can't ⁷_____ in this. It's completely ⁸_____ _____.

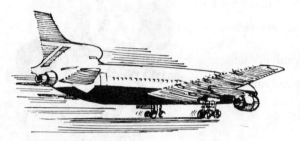

▲ Have you ²_____?
● No, we're OK thanks. Don't stop. Do
  ³_____.

Andrew's alarm clock is ⁴_____, but he is trying to ⁵_____ it _____.

SUSAN   Come and ⁹_____ Rachel, please.

RACHEL But I can't eat cheese. You know the smell always ¹⁰_____ me _____.

PHRASAL VERBS

7.2 Up: Andrew and Rachel

| blow up | get up | put up | wake up |
| break up | grow up | sit up | wind up |

Complete the following, using the verbs shown in the correct tenses.

Andrew has just ¹_____, but he is still sleepy. He is ²_____ in bed, but he doesn't want to ³_____ and get dressed. Actually he hasn't got to, because his school ⁴_____ for the holidays yesterday. Now he is ⁵_____ his watch. He knows that when he is ⁶_____ he won't have nice long school holidays.

Now Andrew and Rachel are getting ready for a party this evening. Rachel is ⁷_____ some decorations, and Andrew is ⁸_____ balloons.

7.3 Prepositional verbs: The suitcase

Look at that suitcase.
Look at it.

look after	laugh at	hope for	belong to
	look at	look for	listen to
		send for	occur to
		wait for	

Complete the following using a different verb from the box in each gap.

TOM Why are you ¹_____ that suitcase like that?

BOB I'm wondering who it ²_____. Perhaps it's got a bomb in it. Did you hear what I said? Are you ³_____ me?

TOM Yes of course, but I must say the idea wouldn't ⁴_____ me. Are you ⁵_____ excitement, or something?

BOB Now you are ⁶_____ me!

TOM No, I'm not. I'm only smiling. But what are you ⁷_____? If you really think it is dangerous, you should report it immediately, and they could ⁸_____ the police.

STRANGER Excuse me. May I have my case? I've been ⁹_____ it everywhere. (He takes the case and goes.)

BOB Really! Why don't people ¹⁰_____ their things better!

42

SECTION 8 VERB PATTERNS

8.1 Verbs of perception: *I saw him run/running*

> He *ran* across the road. ⟶ I *saw him run* across the road.
> He *was running*. ⟶ I *saw him running*.

A detective is questioning a witness about what he has told the police. Complete the dialogue in the way shown, using the pattern *saw him DO* or *saw him DOING*.

1 DETECTIVE You say that this man was hiding in the garden?
   WITNESS   Yes, I saw *him hiding in the garden*.

2 DETECTIVE And then he went towards the house, did he?
   WITNESS   Yes, I saw *him go towards the house*.

3 DETECTIVE Was he running?
   WITNESS   Oh yes, I saw _____

4 DETECTIVE And then he was looking through the windows, you said?
   WITNESS   Yes, I watched _____

5 DETECTIVE And then somebody screamed?
   WITNESS   Yes, I heard _____

6 DETECTIVE Because something was burning?
   WITNESS   Well, yes. I could smell _____

7 DETECTIVE And then smoke was pouring out of the house?
   WITNESS   Yes, I could see _____

8 DETECTIVE What about this other man who was coming up behind you?
   WITNESS   I simply didn't observe _____

9 DETECTIVE Until he suddenly touched you?
   WITNESS   Yes, I felt _____

10 DETECTIVE And then he was putting a cloth over your eyes, you said?
   WITNESS   Yes, I suddenly felt _____

11 DETECTIVE But at this point the fire engine arrived?
   WITNESS   Yes, I heard _____

12 DETECTIVE And the next thing you knew, he was running away very fast?
   WITNESS   Yes, I heard _____

VERB PATTERNS

8.2 Agree to DO, consider DOING

Complete the following by using the correct form – to DO or DOING – of the verb given.

to DO	DOING
agree decide hope manage promise refuse try want can't afford	consider deny keep imagine practise regret stop can't help It's no use

This runner wants (¹ win) _____ the 1500 metres. He is trying (² break) _____ the world record. He doesn't deny (³ feel) _____ anxious before a big race. 'You can't help (⁴ be) _____ nervous at times. But I'll manage (⁵ overcome) _____ my nerves,' he says.

This brilliant ice-skating pair couldn't afford (¹⁰ practise) _____ enough in their early days. But then a big company promised (¹¹ help) _____ if they agreed (¹² advertise) _____ its name. 'We certainly didn't refuse (¹³ do) _____ that. Now we can practise (¹⁴ skate) _____ all the time.'

'I decided (⁶ be) _____ a footballer when I was ten. I never considered (⁷ be) _____ anything else. I've never regretted (⁸ turn) _____ professional. Just imagine (⁹ be) _____ paid to play football!'

This wind-surfer hopes (¹⁵ be) _____ a champion one day. 'I just keep (¹⁶ practise) _____. I've stopped (¹⁷ worry) _____ about falling off. It's no use (¹⁸ worry) _____.'

VERB PATTERNS

8.3 Let, make: What do the notices mean?

Make sentences from the box and use them to explain these notices.

They	let don't let make	you	bring children in. cycle in the park. drive on the left. park free. pay by cheque. pay £1 to enter. pick the flowers. sit at the back of the bus if you smoke. telephone from their shop. walk on the grass.

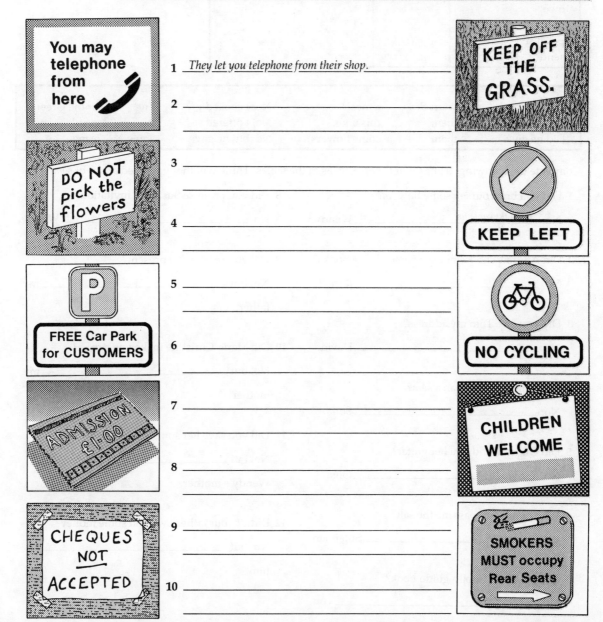

1 They let you telephone from their shop.
2 _____
3 _____
4 _____
5 _____
6 _____
7 _____
8 _____
9 _____
10 _____

45

VERB PATTERNS

8.4 Indirect objects: *to* or *for*?

| buy, choose, cook, find, keep, make, save | it, one, some | for | myself, me, you, Olga, Suleiman |
| give, lend, offer, owe, pass, promise, send | | to | |

Did you cook	yourself	a meal?	No, I cooked	one	*for* the Greens.
Did you offer	them	this book?	No, I offered	it	*to* Suleiman.
Did he give	them	some flowers?	No, but he gave	some	*to* me.

Complete the following, using *for* or *to* correctly as in the tables. Think whether you need *one*, *it* or *some*.

1 Did you buy yourself some flowers?
   No, *I bought some for* _____ Wendy.

2 Did Andrew choose himself some library books?
   No, _____ Rachel.

3 Did you give Tom my address?
   No, _____ David.

4 Did Juan keep Stephan a seat?
   No, _____ Sofia.

5 Did Gudrun lend you her guitar?
   No, _____ Olga.

6 Why didn't you pass me the salt?
   Well, _____ Suleiman.

7 Did you find Minoji a guide-book?
   No, but _____ you.

8 Did you promise Susan an invitation?
   No, _____ Wendy.

9 Did you send Bob a present?
   No, but _____ my father.

10 Did Marie-Christine make you a cake?
   No, but _____ my mother.

11 Did you save her some strawberries?
   No, but _____ Wendy's mother.

12 Didn't your father owe you some money?
   No, but _____ him!

VERB PATTERNS

8.5 Infinitives: *Careers*

Suleiman is studying *to become a doctor*. *To pass her engineering exams* Gudrun has got to work hard.	**Purpose**
Learning languages will give Olga the chance *to work abroad*. Visiting England is a good way *to improve your English*.	**Noun + *to* infinitive**

A Complete this letter with *to* infinitives. Use these verbs:

| apply | ask | continue | do | get | improve | pass | see | talk | work |

Dear Sir,
　　I am writing _____(1) if you can help me. I am at present studying _____(2) my school exams, and working hard _____(3) my English. Next year, if it is possible, I would like to go abroad _____(4) my studies. But _____(5) this, I need money, so I am wondering if you can advise me the best way _____(6) a grant. And can you tell me please — do I have to be over eighteen _____(7) for one?
　　I would welcome an opportunity _____(8) to you if you have the time _____(9) me.
　　Of course, I intend to return to this country _____(10) at the end of my studies.
　　　　　　　　　　Yours faithfully,

VERB PATTERNS

To be a good writer, To become a ski instructor, To be a teacher, To work in a travel agency, To succeed in banking,	you have to . . .

B *More careers.* What do you have to do to be good in a career? Here is what some of the students say. Can you match them up?

11 _____ you have to like children.

12 _____ you have to be good at sums.

13 _____ you have to know a lot of geography.

14 _____ you have to like an outdoor life.

15 _____ you have to love words.

C *A questionnaire.* Ask your friends to answer the following three questions by choosing the most important reason each time (a, b, or c). Put a tick (✓) in 1a for each person who says the most important reason why people work is to make money – and so on.

1 Why do people work?	a to make money	
	b to occupy their time	
	c to lead useful lives	
2 Why do people take foreign holidays?	a to visit famous places	
	b to find out how other people live	
	c to collect souvenirs	
3 What are you learning English for?	a to please (our) parents	
	b to be able to talk to foreigners	
	c to get a better job	

Now complete this.

1 A lot of/Most of my friends think that people work _____

2 We think that people take foreign holidays _____

3 Most of us are learning English _____

SECTION 9 COMPLEX SENTENCES

9.1 True conditions: *Snakes and ladders*

A Can you explain the rules of *Snakes and Ladders*? Remember, you shake the dice and go forward the same number of squares that you have thrown. And you go up ladders and down snakes. (As the rules are always the same, we use present tenses.)

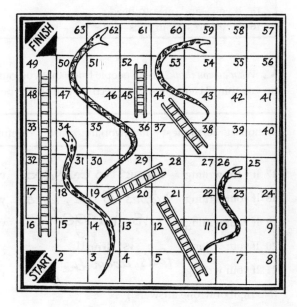

1 If you __land__ on the bottom of a ladder, you __go up__ it.

2 If you __land__ on the top of a ladder, you __stay__ there.

3 If you _____ on the head of a snake, you _____ it.

4 If you _____ on the tail of a snake, you _____ there.

5 So, if you throw six to start, you _____ on 6 and go up to 21.

6 Then, if you _____ five, you _____ on 26 and you _____ to 11.

7 If you now _____ five again, you _____ on 16 and you _____ to 49.

8 If you now _____ three, you _____ on 52, and you _____ there.

9 If you now _____ four, you _____ on 56, and you _____ there.

10 If you now _____ three, you _____ on 59, and you _____.

Bad luck! Where are you? ☐

49

COMPLEX SENTENCES

B Here are some more things that are always true. Can you sort them out?

11	If you mix red and yellow	a	you don't walk upside down.
12	If there's no air	b	the blood rushes to your head.
13	If water is heated to 100°C	c	you see red.
14	If you live in Australia	d	you can't breathe.
15	If you stand on your head	e	you get orange.
16	If you press your eyes hard	f	it boils.

C *What do you think?* Some people think that you can tell people's characters from their handwriting. What do you think? Here are some adjectives to describe people. Complete the sentences with some of them.

honest   dishonest   hardworking   lazy   careful   careless   kind   unkind   friendly   unfriendly

17 If your writing *slopes to the left* you are _____
18 If your writing *slopes to the right* you are _____
19 If your writing *is large* you _____
20 If your writing *is small* you _____
21 If your writing *falls down the page* you _____

(No right or wrong answers!)

9.2 Conditions: *Future possibilities*

Write two conditional sentences for each box. We have done the first one for you.

? fine tomorrow	✓	go swimming
	✗	go to the cinema

1a *If it's fine tomorrow, I'll go swimming.*

1b *If it isn't fine, I'll go to the cinema.*

? have enough money	✓	buy a cassette player
	✗	not buy one

2a _____

2b _____

COMPLEX SENTENCES

? eat too much	✓	get fat
	✗	stay slim

3a _____

3b _____

? pass my exams next year	✓	go up to the next class
	✗	have to take them again

4a _____

4b _____

? win a prize	✓	be delighted
	✗	not be surprised!

5a _____

5b _____

? telephone my grandmother this evening	✓	tell her all my news
	✗	have to write to her

6a _____

6b _____

? work harder	✓	my parents/be pleased
	✗	my parents/be cross

7a _____

7b _____

COMPLEX SENTENCES

9.3 Conditions: *If only things were different now!*

> 'If I *were(was)* grown up, I *could please* myself.' SHE IS NOT GROWN UP. SHE CAN'T PLEASE HERSELF.
> 'If I *didn't have to* come to school every day, I *wouldn't come*.' SHE HAS TO COME TO SCHOOL EVERY DAY.

A Rachel is day-dreaming – if only things were different! Here are some more facts about Rachel. Write down what she is thinking.

1 She is a child. She has to come to school.
   If I weren't a child, I wouldn't have to come to school.

2 She is not a princess. She doesn't live in a palace.

3 She hasn't got wings. She cannot fly away like a bird.

4 She has to come to school. She is not free!

5 She can't play tennis well. She can't be a world champion.

6 The work is so difficult. She has to spend so much time on it.

7 They don't live in a really hot country. They don't go swimming every day.

8 She does not really understand French. She can't do it.

B *What about you?* Do you sometimes think 'If only things were different'? Complete the following about yourself.

9 I am not _____
   If I were _____, I would _____

10 I don't like _____
   If I _____, I _____

11 I can't _____
   If I _____, I _____

12 My class has to _____
   If we _____, we _____

52

COMPLEX SENTENCES

9.4 Wishing: *She wishes things were different now*

> Rachel wishes she *were(was)* a princess.   SHE IS *NOT* A PRINCESS.
> She wishes she *lived* in a palace.   SHE *DOES NOT* LIVE IN A PALACE.
> She wishes she *didn't live* in an ordinary house.   SHE *LIVES* IN AN ORDINARY HOUSE.

A Complete the following, saying what Rachel wishes.

1 She has to come to school.
   She wishes she didn't have to come to school.

2 She hasn't got wings.

3 She is not free.

4 She can't play tennis well.

5 The work is so difficult.

6 She and Andrew don't live in a really hot country.

7 They don't go swimming every day.

8 She has to spend so much time on her work.

B *What about you?* Write down some things that you, and the people you know, wish were different now.

9 I wish _____
10 My friend wishes _____
11 We all wish that we _____
12 My brother/sister wishes _____
13 My father and mother wish _____
14 Our neighbours wish _____
15 _____
16 _____

53

COMPLEX SENTENCES

9.5 Wishing about the future: *Things could be different one day*

Wishing for ourselves				
I We	wish	I we	could	become ... buy ... go ... learn ... leave ...

A Here is Andrew speaking. Complete what he says, using the table.

1 I haven't got a radio transmitter.

   _____ one some time.

2 I've never been to India.

   _____ there one day.

3 My parents say hang-gliding is dangerous.

   But _____

4 My friends and I are still at school.

   We _____ soon.

5 I love flying.

   _____ a pilot.

Wishing about other people			
I wish	you he she they	could (n't) would (n't)	come ... hurry ... see ... telephone ... tidy ...

B And here is Susan. Complete what she is thinking or saying, using the table.

6 (Rachel and Andrew's rooms are untidy.) I wish they would _____ them.

7 Rachel! Andrew! You're being very slow. _____ you two would _____.

8 I wonder where Bob is. _____ would _____ me.

9 (Wendy and David have said that they can't come to dinner on Saturday.) What a pity. I _____ you could _____.

10 (The dentist can see Susan tomorrow – but she doesn't want to go!) I wish _____ me tomorrow.

54

COMPLEX SENTENCES

9.6 More relative clauses

> I like that TV detective. He always solves all his problems.
> → I like that TV detective *who* always solves all his problems.
>
> I've seen lots of films. I've really enjoyed them.
> → I've seen lots of films I've really enjoyed.

Join the following pairs of sentences together, so that the second is a relative clause (as in the examples in the box). Practise using *who* (for people) and *that* (for things) where relative pronouns are necessary – but leave gaps where this is possible.

1 Who was that actor? He played Superman. *Who was that actor who played Superman?*

2 What was that film about a shark? The shark terrorized people for years. _____

3 What was the name of that actress? She became Princess Grace of Monaco. _____

4 Star Wars is a film. You really must see it. _____

5 'Beverly Hills Cop' and 'Trading Places' were two Eddie Murphy films. They amused me very much. _____

6 The Beatles were four young men from Liverpool. They became world-famous. _____

7 Liverpool is a city in northern England. Most tourists never visited it. _____

8 But now there are guided tours. You can take them round Liverpool. _____

9 Elvis Presley was a great pop star. Everyone has heard of him. _____

10 Joan Armatrading is a singer. People admire her today. _____

11 I've got lots of cassettes. They remind me of my favourite films. _____

12 Barbra Streisand is an actress. I'm sure you have seen her. _____

COMPLEX SENTENCES

9.7 Relative clauses with prepositions at the end

Can you define the words below from the clues? We have done the first one for you. Notice how the answers end with prepositions.

Clues (not in order)
You climb up and down them.
You can keep money in one.
You can open tins with one.
You can sit on one or lean against it.
You can sleep in one.

You fasten papers together with them.
You pour liquids from them.
People spend too long looking at them.
Swimmers and divers jump off them.

Definitions

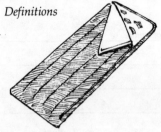

1 A sleeping bag is something *you can sleep in.*

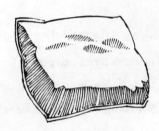

2 A cushion is something

3 A paper clip is a little metal thing

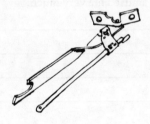

4 A tin-opener is a thing

5 A springboard is something

6 A jug is something

7 A purse is a sort of little bag

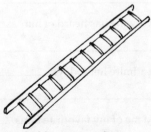

8 A ladder is something

9 A television set is a 'box'

9.8 Relative clauses: *who, which, whose*

> *a little village*
>
> *It*'s a favourite of mine.
> → This is a little village *which* is a favourite of mine.
>
> You could never pronounce *its* name.
> → This is a little village *whose* name you could never pronounce.
>
> *some friends*
>
> *They* write to me regularly.
> → These are some friends *who* write to me regularly.
>
> *Their* farmhouse is a hundred years old.
> → These are some friends *whose* farmhouse is a hundred years old.

Olga is showing photographs of Poland. What does she say about the photographs? Use *This is/These are* and *who/which/whose*.

1 a village. Its name is Wloszczowa.

   This is a village whose name is Wloszczowa.

2 an aunt of mine. Her family have lived there for 300 years.

   _____

3 some friends. I've often stayed on their farm.

   _____

4 a part of Poland. This part has a very good climate.

   _____

5 some people. They were staying there last year.

   _____

6 a city. This city always interests visitors.

   _____

7 a hotel. It is very good value.

   _____

8 the aunt. She gave me my cassette player.

   _____

9 a friend. She is coming to visit me soon.

   _____

10 a church. It has lovely windows.

   _____

COMPLEX SENTENCES

9.9 What to do: A crash survivor

> They would not know *where they ought to look*.
> → *where to look*.
> She had no idea *which way she should go*.
> → *which way to go*.

Read this extraordinary true story, and then change the underlined words into *wh-word + to + verb*, as in the examples above.

On 24th December 1971, a plane carrying 92 passengers crashed in the Amazon jungle. Only one person, a teenage German girl, Juliane Koepcke, survived. She found herself, still in her plane seat, on the ground with dead bodies on top of her, and with her legs and back badly hurt.

She knew that if people looked for survivors, (1) they would not know *where they ought to look*. So (2) she decided *what she was going to do*. She was going to find a river, because somewhere down a river there must be people. But (3) she did not know *where she should look for one*. (4) She had no idea *which way she should go*. For hours – perhaps days – she walked. Then, she found a river. Luckily (5) she knew *how she could make a simple raft*, and on this she floated down the river.

(6) There was no problem knowing *when she ought to sleep*. She fell asleep when she was tired. But terrible worms crawled into her wounds, and (7) it was difficult to know *how she could get them out*. (8) Another big problem was *what she could eat*. For three days she lived on a cake which she had had with her in the plane. After that (9) she was not sure *which plants she could eat safely* and (10) *which she must avoid*. For a whole week she ate nothing, but slowly – ill and alone – she continued her journey. Ten days after the crash Juliane Koepcke came out of the jungle. An amazingly brave teenager.

1 They would not know _____
2 She decided _____
3 She did not know _____
4 She had no idea _____
5 She knew _____
6 There was no problem knowing _____
7 It was difficult to know _____
8 Another big problem was _____
9 She was not sure _____
10 – and _____

58